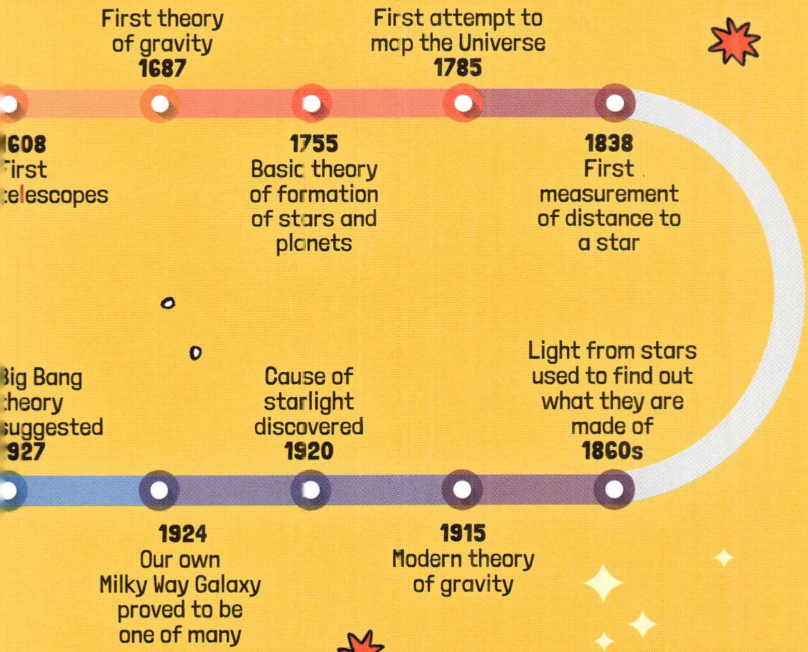

1608
First
telescopes
First theory
of gravity
1687
1755
Basic theory
of formation
of stars and
planets
First attempt to
map the Universe
1785
1838
First
measurement
of distance to
a star
Light from stars
used to find out
what they are
made of
1860s
1915
Modern theory
of gravity
Cause of
starlight
discovered
1920
1924
Our own
Milky Way Galaxy
proved to be
one of many
Big Bang
theory
suggested
1927

VERY SHORT INTRODUCTIONS FOR CURIOUS YOUNG MINDS

The SECRETS of the UNIVERSE

Dr. Mike Goldsmith

OXFORD
UNIVERSITY PRESS

OXFORD
UNIVERSITY PRESS

Great Clarendon Street, Oxford OX2 6DP

Oxford University Press is a department of the University of Oxford. It furthers the University's objective of excellence in research, scholarship, and education by publishing worldwide. Oxford is a registered trade mark of Oxford University Press in the UK and in certain other countries

Text written by Dr. Mike Goldsmith
Illustrated by Adam Quest and Ana Seixas

Designed and edited by Raspberry Books Ltd

The moral rights of the author have been asserted

Database right Oxford University Press (maker)

First published 2022
This hardback edition published 2025

Library of Congress Cataloging-in-Publication

Data is available

ISBN 978-1-382-07042-3

1 3 5 7 9 10 8 6 4 2

The manufacturing process conforms to the environmental regulations of the country of origin.

Printed in China

The manufacturer's authorised representative in the EU for product safety is Oxford University Press España S.A. of El Parque Empresarial San Fernando de Henares, Avenida de Castilla, 2 – 28830 Madrid (www.oup.es/en or product.safety@oup.com). OUP España S.A. also acts as importer into Spain of products made by the manufacturer.

Acknowledgments

The publisher and authors would like to thank the following for permission to use photographs and other copyright material:

Cover artwork: Adam Quest and Ana Seixas. Photos: Pavlo S/Shutterstock. **Inside photos:** p1(tl): Pavlo S/Shutterstock; p12: Nicku/Shutterstock; p17: Webspark/Shutterstock; p24 (from left to right): cobalt88/Shutterstock; itsmejust/Shutterstock; Minerva Studio/Shutterstock; p25: NASA/ESA; p37: Designua/Shutterstock; p41(t): Volodymyr Goinyk/ Shutterstock; p41(ml): D1min/Shutterstock; p41(mr): K.K.T Madhusanka/Shutterstock; p41 (from top left): Fotyma/Shutterstock; azure1/Shutterstock; Hedzun Vasyl/Shutterstock; miha de/Shutterstock; Catmando/ Shutterstock; Andrea Danti/Shutterstock; creativemarc/ Shutterstock; p43(t): antb/Shutterstock; p43(b): Trifonenkolvan/Shutterstock; p44: NASA, ESA, and M. Livio and the Hubble 20th Anniversary Team (STScI); p51: Uzono Studio/Shutterstock; p52(1): ESA/Hubble & NASA, A. Riess et al., M. Zamani; p52(2): ESA/Hubble & NASA; p52(3): ESA/Hubble & NASA, Flickr user Det58; p52(4): NASA, ESA, and The Hubble Heritage Team (STScI/AURA); p52(5): NASA, ESA; acknowledgment: T. Roberts (Durham University, UK), D. Calzetti (University of Massachusetts) and the LEGUS Team, R. Tully (University of Hawaii) and R. Chandar (University of Toledo); p52(6): NASA, ESA, the Hubble Heritage (STScI/AURA)-ESA/Hubble Collaboration, and A. Evans (University of Virginia, Charlottesville/NRAO/ Stony Brook University); p53: ESA/Hubble & NASA, A. Seth; p58: Event Horizon Telescope Collaboration et al.; p75: NASA/CXC/SAO; p77: John Ebersole, APOD, May 16, 2016; p78: NASA/JPL-Caltech; p89: NASA/ JPL-Caltech. **Front end paper:** pp2-3: Aleksandr Bryliaev/Shutterstock. **Back end paper:** p2: Pavlo S/ Shutterstock.

Author photo courtesy of Dr. Mike Goldsmith

Artwork by **Adam Quest**, **Ana Seixas**, Ekaterina Gorelova, Geraldine Sy, Aaron Cushley, Esteban Hernández, Raspberry Books, Q2A Media Services Pvt. Ltd, and Oxford University Press.

Every effort has been made to contact copyright holders of material reproduced in this book. Any omissions will be rectified in subsequent printings if notice is given to the publisher.

Contents

Chapter 1. What is the Universe? **4**

Chapter 2. Discovering the Universe **9**

Chapter 3. Studying Space **16**

Chapter 4. The Universe's Biggest Secret **33**

Chapter 5. The Lives of the Stars **42**

Chapter 6. Our Place in the Universe **50**

Chapter 7. Since the Beginning **63**

Chapter 8. The End of the Universe **81**

Chapter 9. Cosmic Mysteries **88**

Distances from Earth **92**

Glossary **92**

Index **95**

Chapter 1

What is the Universe?

The Universe is everything that exists, or ever did, or ever will.

Almost everything about the Universe is huge, including its size, its age, and the number of stars it contains. It's so enormous that we need special units of measurement to talk about it. The best known is the **light year**.

Shorter distances can be measured in light days, light minutes, or light seconds. Even a light second is a huge distance: The distance around Earth's equator is only about a seventh of a light second. The Moon is just over a light second away, the Sun about eight light minutes, the nearest star around four light years, and the distance across the Universe is thousands of millions of light years.

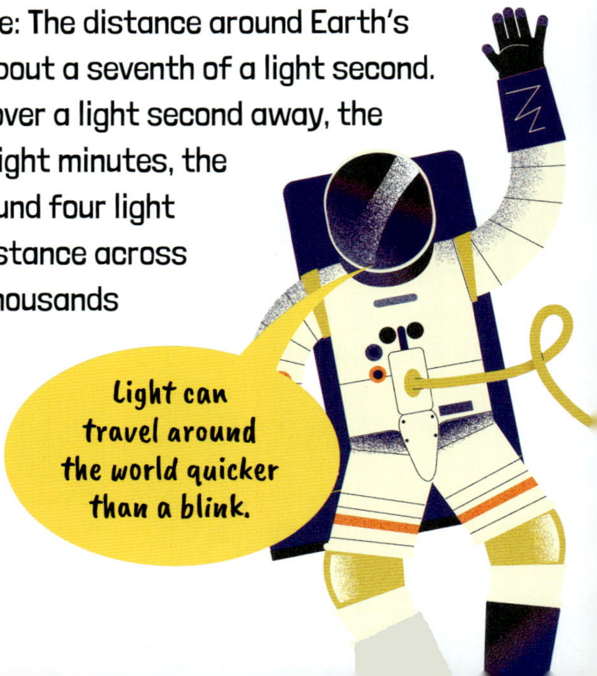

Speak like a **scientist**

COSMOLOGY

"**Cosmology**" means the study of the Universe, and the people who do the studying are called "cosmologists." "Cosmos" is another word for the Universe, which comes from the Ancient Greek word "kosmos," meaning "world." The "-ology" part also comes from Ancient Greek—the word "logia," which means "study of."

LIGHT YEAR

One light year is the distance light can travel in a year. Light travels so fast (186,000 miles per second) that a light year is a very long way, nearly six trillion miles. If we look at a star which is, say, ten light years away, we see it as it was ten years ago—because the light from the star has taken ten years to travel ten light years. So looking at stars and **galaxies** means looking back in time. Since a lot of cosmology is about studying the history of the Universe, this is very useful.

The Universe is ancient: about

13.8 billion (13,800,000,000) years old.

And it contains many stars, perhaps a billion **trillion** (1000,000,000,000,000,000,000) of them. These numbers all refer to the "observable" Universe—that is, the parts of the Universe that we could see, in theory, with the best possible telescopes. It is a huge sphere, billions of light years across, with us in the middle. There might be stars and other objects beyond this sphere, but we can't see them. That's because light traveling from them would take longer than the Universe has existed to reach us.

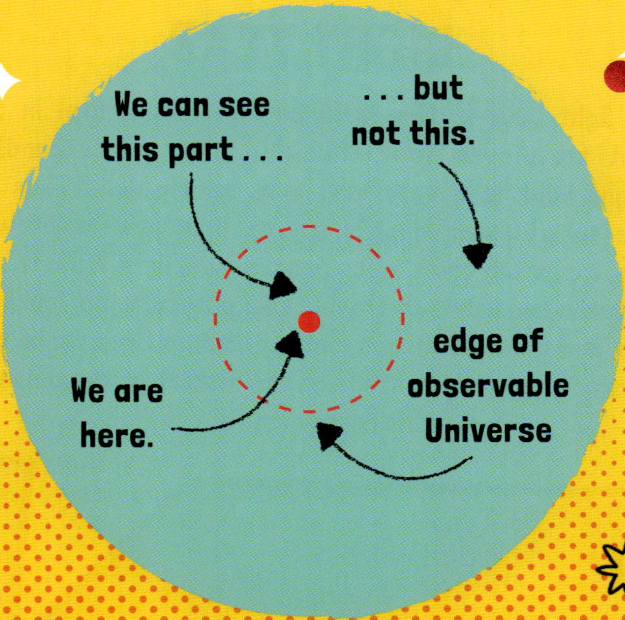

The simple Universe

Most of the Universe is made up of hydrogen and helium, gathered up by **gravity** in enormous amounts to form stars (which are themselves mostly gathered into groups called galaxies) and gas clouds. This leaves space almost empty, and so clear that we can see right through it across the Universe.

When cosmologists look through this wonderfully clear space, they see that every part of the Universe is very similar to the part where we live: Even the most distant stars are made of the same things as nearby ones and have very similar structures and lives.

As far as the Universe (and cosmologists) are concerned, Earth and the other planets of our **Solar System** are so small that they're barely worth a second thought. Our most powerful rockets and fastest space probes have only explored a tiny part of space around us, so you won't find them in this book. We're mostly going to concentrate on the bigger picture—the vast Universe as a whole.

This is a very short introduction to the Universe and its secrets. You'll discover that . . .

The Universe is expanding.

It contains over a trillion trillion planets.

A whole lot happened in the Universe's first three minutes.

Most of it is invisible.

Stars work like bicycle pumps.

No one understands what most of it is.

Read on to find out some of the secrets of the Universe . . .

Chapter 2

Discovering the Universe

To you and me, the word "Universe" suggests a vast space, full of bright stars. But our ancestors had very different ideas.

Ancient ideas

Today, we know that there is nothing special about our place in the Universe: Our Sun is just an ordinary star, and Earth is a very average planet. But ancient people had no reason to think the stars were anything like the Sun and assumed that they were small and near—just above the clouds, perhaps. Because the Sun crosses the sky by day, and the stars do the same thing by night, they assumed the Sun and stars were moving while Earth remained still.

These long-ago people noticed that the noonday Sun is highest in the sky in the summer and lowest in winter, different patterns of stars are visible at different times of year, and the Moon goes through a pattern of changes of shape every 29½ days. So, the sky could tell people what time of year it was.

Calendars were invented based on the Sun or the Moon. The Sun and Moon were so useful, as well as bright and beautiful, that many people worshipped them as gods.

Some skywatchers were fascinated by five bright stars that shifted their position each night. Now we know these are planets, like Earth, but then they were thought to be special stars—or maybe yet more gods.

Until the twentieth century, most people thought that the Universe was created by a god, or several gods, thousands of years ago. Some thought that it was made from the silt at the bottom of an endless ocean, some thought it hatched from an egg.

The beliefs of these ancient people still influence the way we talk about the sky today: The nearby planets and the brighter stars have names that were given to them thousands of years ago, and the ancient names of the patterns that stars make in the sky, called **constellations**, are mostly still in use.

the planet Mars, named after the Roman god of war

The constellations **Orion the hunter** and **Pegasus the flying horse** are from ancient Greek mythology.

A heavenly revolution

The ancient Greeks were the first to try to understand the stars and planets. They developed theories to make sense of them, some of which were correct, like Aristarchus's theory that Earth and the planets move around the Sun. The ideas of Aristotle were the most widely accepted by later civilizations. Unfortunately, most of them were wrong—such as the idea that Earth is the center of the Universe, and that the Sun, stars, and planets are made of a substance not found on Earth.

There wasn't much progress until **1543**, when a Polish **astronomer** called Nicolaus Copernicus died, and that same year his masterpiece was published. It was written in Latin, but in English its title is *On the Revolutions of the Heavenly Spheres*. In it, Copernicus suggested that Earth and the other planets revolve around the Sun, just as Aristarchus had thought. The book was so important, and became so famous, that we use the word "revolution" from its title to mean an overthrow of existing ways and beliefs.

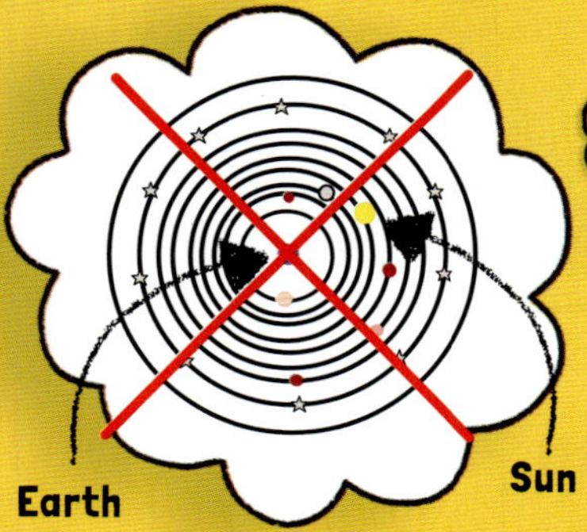

HEROES OF THE UNIVERSE

NICOLAUS COPERNICUS

Helped prove Earth goes around the Sun.

HEROES OF THE UNIVERSE

GALILEO GALILEI

Built and used the first astronomical telescope and helped prove that Copernicus was correct.

The theory of Copernicus and Aristarchus is called "heliocentric," which means sun-centered (Aristotle's Earth-centered theory is called "geocentric": "helio" means "Sun" and "geo" means "Earth"). The heliocentric theory was finally accepted mostly because of the work of the great Italian astronomer and scientist Galileo Galilei. In 1609, he built one of the world's first telescopes, and looking through it he discovered that the planet Jupiter has moons revolving around it, proving that not everything orbits Earth as Aristotle had claimed.

The Solar System

The Sun and planets' sizes are roughly to scale, but their distances aren't. If they were, this book would be half a mile wide, which would need a ridiculously large bookcase.

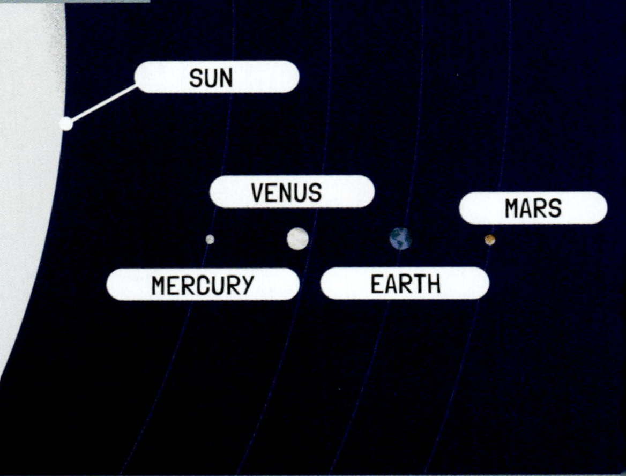

Speak like a scientist

SOLAR SYSTEM

The Sun and all the many kinds of objects that go around it, including planets, comets, dust, and gases, make up the Solar System. Earth is the third planet from the Sun. Although the outermost planet (Neptune) is just over four light hours from the Sun, there are many tiny objects beyond, stretching to a distance of at least a light year. When other stars have planets and other objects going around them, these are called **planetary systems.**

Gradually, other astronomers realized that there is a lot more to the Universe than the Solar System and a few thousand stars. German-British astronomer William Herschel discovered a new planet, Uranus,

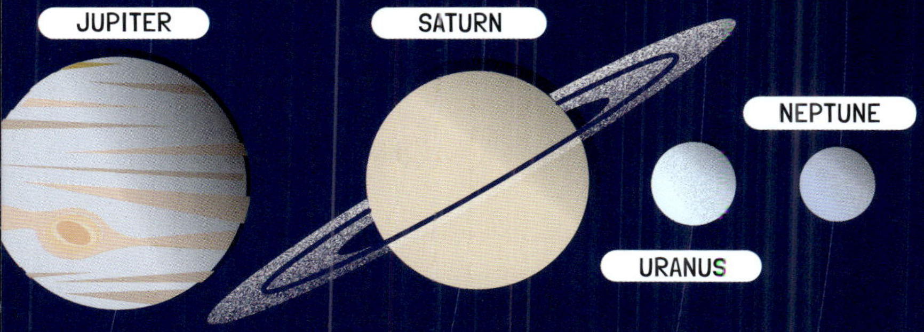

in 1785, and he was also the first person to try to make a map of the entire Universe. Even though his telescopes (which he built himself) were the best in the world, they could not see very far into space, so his map of the Universe actually only covers a small part of our galaxy and is not very accurate either. But it was a great leap forward toward our modern understanding that Earth, and everything we can see around it, is just a tiny fragment of a vast Universe of stars.

Cosmology hadn't really got started, because no one even knew the most basic things about the Universe yet.

But, thanks to scientists and inventors, that was

all about to change,

as the next chapter will explain . . .

Chapter 3

Studying Space

Since the days of the ancient Greeks, astronomers had been certain that the planets move in circles around either the Sun or Earth.

It's odd that they were so certain, because the way the planets move across the sky doesn't fit this idea. Finally, in 1604, German astronomer Johannes Kepler realized that planets actually go around the Sun along shapes called ellipses (ovals). He also found that they move faster the closer they are to the Sun. Later, he published his discoveries, now called Kepler's Laws.

HEROES OF THE UNIVERSE

JOHANNES KEPLER

Founded the laws describing the motions of the planets.

But to go further and find out why, rather than how, the planets move as they do, better science was needed. Luckily, the age of modern science was just beginning.

These are some of the most important breakthroughs:

1 In the 1660s, British physicist Isaac Newton showed that gravity operated throughout the Solar System as well as on Earth. He also worked out the mathematical laws that describe the way objects move. Together, these two discoveries explained the motions of the planets that Kepler had worked out. Newton also found that the white light of the Sun can be separated into a rainbow of blurred colors called a **spectrum**, by using a shaped piece of glass called a prism.

HEROES OF THE UNIVERSE

ISAAC NEWTON

Mathematician and physicist who discovered the laws of motion and gravity, and that white light is a mix of colors.

Speak like a **scientist**

GRAVITY

Gravity is what pulls a ball back to Earth when you throw it and holds the Solar System together. Every object in the Universe attracts every other object with the pull of gravity, which depends on just two things: **mass** (which we feel as weight) and distance. Two massive objects that are close together attract each other strongly, while the attraction between low mass or distant objects is weak.

2 In 1800, William Herschel discovered that there is more to the spectrum of sunlight than color. Just beyond the red end is an area of warmth. The warmth is due to infrared, which we can't see. Before long, it was found that there is also something just beyond the violet end of the spectrum—ultraviolet, which can burn our skin if we're not careful. Together, visible light, infrared, and ultraviolet are called **radiation** (part of the **electromagnetic spectrum**, which we'll meet later on).

Radiation sort of behaves like waves on the sea. The length of the waves is what gives light its color: Red light has longer waves than violet.

3 By the end of the eighteenth century, scientists, together with the engineers and inventors who developed the steam engines that were rapidly changing the world, showed that heat, light, sound, motion, and similar things could change into each other. This group of things is called **energy**.

4 Meanwhile, experiments with electricity and magnetism led to the invention of electric motors and generators, and to the discovery of yet another kind of radiation: radio waves, which are much longer than light waves. The shortest radio waves are called microwaves, and these turned out to be very important for cosmologists later on.

5 In the early twentieth century, Albert Einstein discovered that mass (which is closely related to weight) is a kind of energy; a discovery that would lead scientists to work out how stars shine. He also realized that energy, time, and space are closely related, and explained gravity in a new way, as we'll see.

He used these ideas to develop theories about **the whole Universe.**

HEROES OF THE UNIVERSE

ALBERT EINSTEIN

In 1916 he published his theory of General Relativity, which explained the nature of gravity, and then, in 1917, published a theory of the whole Universe based on it. Both theories are still accepted today.

Sun and stars

On a clear and moonless night, far from artificial lights, you can see more than a thousand stars. But even with the light from so many stars, the night is still very dark, so it's hard to believe that each star is as bright as our Sun (more or less). We only know stars are so bright because we know how distant they are, but it took centuries of effort to measure these distances.

The Universe up close

Until Galilei peered through his telescope, humans were limited by their eyesight to a very tiny part of the Universe. But since then, bigger and better telescopes have been invented, revealing millions of stars and many other objects.

Telescopes make things look closer and brighter, and there are two main types: Those like Galileo's use a lens to bend ("refract") the light of distant objects and are called refractors. Binoculars are pairs of refractors.

Refracting telescope

Reflecting telescope

Reflecting telescopes use a large, curved mirror to do the job. Isaac Newton built the world's first reflector in 1668, and today the most powerful telescopes are reflectors.

Telescopes were soon being fitted with instruments to map infrared and ultraviolet as well as light, because stars also produce these kinds of radiation. Stars produce radio waves too, but to detect these, a new kind of telescope had to be developed. These use huge metal dishes to gather radio waves.

Radio telescope

During the late twentieth century, all these new radiations, powerful telescopes, sensitive detectors, and some nifty mathematics were used together to reveal a vast and complex new Universe.

The electromagnetic spectrum

Visible light, infrared, ultraviolet, and radio waves are all parts of the electromagnetic spectrum. Albert Einstein and his colleagues showed that light and the other kinds of radiation, though most simply understood as waves, can be better explained as being made of tiny particles called photons. The only difference between various kinds of radiation is the energy of an individual photon: An ultraviolet photon has hundreds of millions of times the energy of a radio photon.

By the end of the twentieth century, even more types of radiation had been discovered, including X-rays (used to look inside the body) and gamma rays (produced in **nuclear** explosions). The first space missions found that stars and other objects in space produce these too.

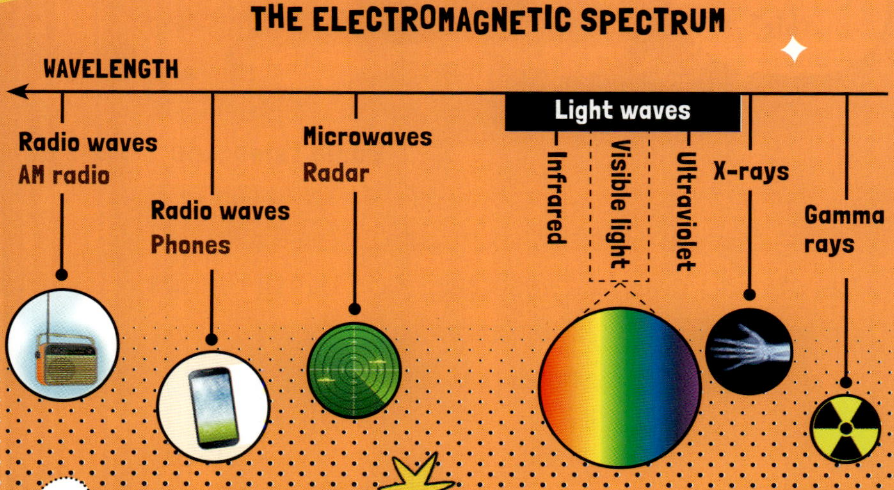

Fortunately for us, Earth's atmosphere shields us from most of these dangerous kinds of radiation, as well as some ultraviolet and infrared.

Because these types of radiation can't be observed from Earth, telescopes had to be sent into space to study them.

The most famous of these space telescopes, the Hubble Space Telescope (HST), collects light and infrared using a mirror. Although the mirror is smaller than those of many Earth telescopes, its view is never blocked by clouds or haze. And it can look at the same very faint star or other object for many days on end, gradually building up an image photon by photon. In this way, the HST has revealed parts of the Universe billions of light years away (and therefore billions of years ago).

Image of deep space taken by Hubble Space Telescope

Gravitational waves

In addition to telescopes, astronomers have another kind of instrument, which they use to detect gravitational waves. These aren't part of the electromagnetic spectrum, they are disturbances in space that are produced by any object when it speeds up, slows down, or changes direction. But they are so weak that only the most dramatic events in the Universe—like **black holes** colliding with each other or swallowing up stars—can be detected by today's gravitational wave detectors. One day, cosmologists expect to be able to detect gravitational waves generated very soon after the beginning of the Universe.

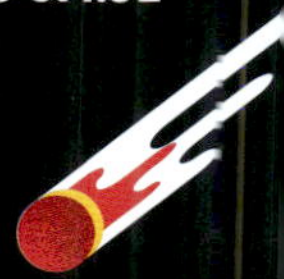

Hidden in starlight

In most areas of science, investigating something—like a rock, a plant, or a disease—begins by making many kinds of measurements and then carrying out experiments. In this way, scientists collect all kinds of data (information) to analyze. But, unlike other scientists, cosmologists have no way to reach the things they study: A few Earth spacecraft are already on their way to other stars, having completed their missions to study the outer planets of the Solar System, but they won't pass by any stars for many thousands of years—and by then, those stars might possibly have been reached by humans. How this might happen is unimaginable to us, but then, a couple of thousand years ago (or even a couple of hundred), reaching the Moon was just as unimaginable, and no one had any real idea how to do it.

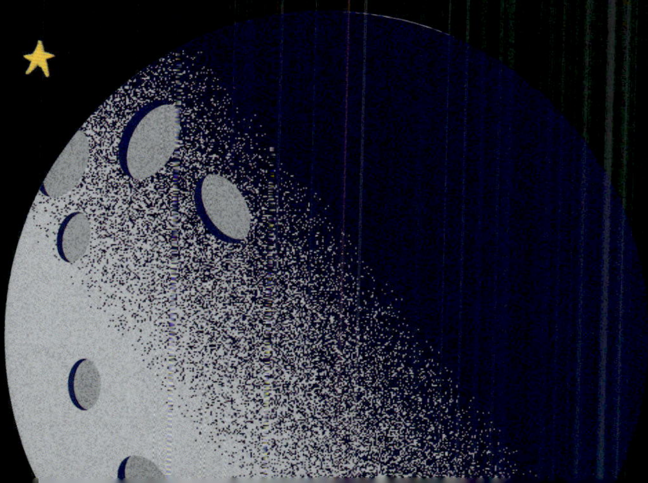

So, cosmologists must make do with very few sources of data—almost all they have is starlight. Amazingly, and luckily, starlight tells us nearly everything about a star, from what it is made of to how fast it is moving.

In 1802, William Hyde Wollaston found a way to produce a sharper version of the Sun's spectrum and noticed that its bands of color are crossed by black lines, now called spectral lines.

A modern image of the **Sun's spectrum** showing spectral lines

Decades later, other scientists found similar lines in the spectra (spectra is the plural of spectrum) made by the flames of many materials including hydrogen, iron, sodium, and calcium, when they are burned. This means that the Sun must contain those materials.

A new science, spectroscopy, had been born and was soon being applied to the stars to find out what they are made of.

Meanwhile, in 1842, Christian Doppler discovered a simple but useful fact about light waves, now called the **Doppler Effect**, which actually works for sound waves as well. If you listen to the sound of a siren on a fire truck as it passes you, it will change from high-pitched to low-pitched.

Light does something very similar.

If a glowing object like a star is rushing away from you at great speed, its light waves will be **stretched**, which means it will appear redder (because it is the wavelength of light that gives it its color—see page 19). If the object is rushing toward you, it will be bluer. (The object is said to be **redshifted** or **blueshifted**.)

This effect is usually so slight that we don't notice it. However, the wavelengths of spectral lines can be measured very accurately. If a star or other glowing object in space is moving away from us, the Doppler Effect means the wavelengths of all its spectral lines get a little longer, shifting toward the red end of the spectrum, and this change tells us the speed of the star.

When a star moves away from us, the wavelengths of the lines in its spectrum get bigger, moving toward the red end of the spectrum. That is, they are redshifted . . .

. . . compared to the lines of a star that isn't moving:

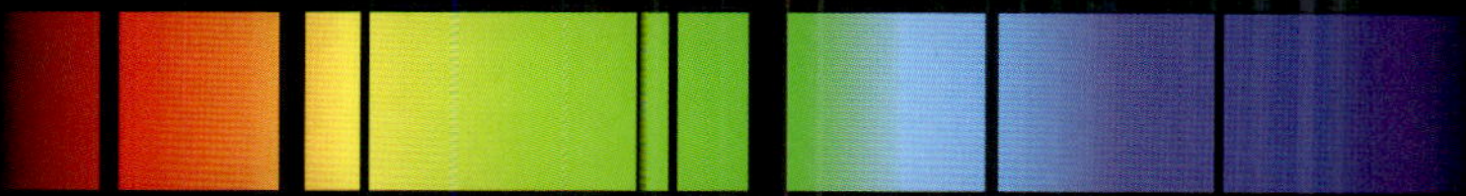

A star moving toward us is blueshifted:

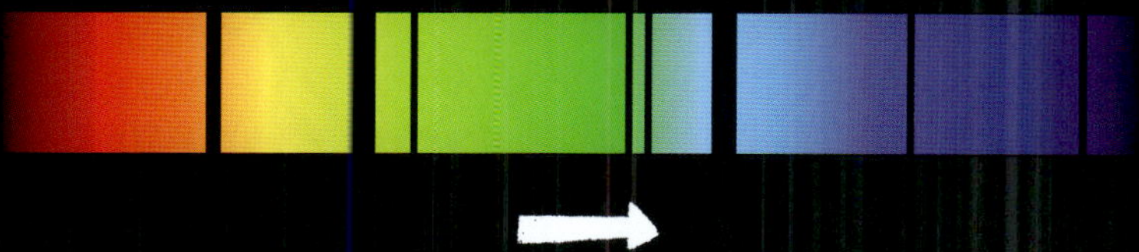

The amount of shift tells us the star's speed.

By the 1880s, astronomers had noticed that some stars have very similar patterns of spectral lines to one another, and a team led by Edward Pickering used spectra to classify stars. Members of his team were Williamina Fleming, Annie Jump Cannon, Antonia Maury, and Florence Cushman. Their system is still used today.

Now that astronomers could work out how bright and hot a star is, and what it is made of, they could combine this with their knowledge of the way **atoms** release energy to tell the stories of the stars. But before those stories can be told, the Universe has an amazing secret to reveal . . .

Chapter 4

The Universe's Biggest Secret

In 1919, there were two new arrivals at the Mount Wilson Observatory in Canada: one was keen young astronomer Edwin Hubble, the other was the shiny new Hooker telescope with its huge eight-foot mirror. Together, they discovered the true scale of the Universe and helped unlock its biggest secret.

Hubble was interested in what were then called spiral **nebulae**: faint cloudy patterns of light with distinctive curving shapes.

To study them, he used Henrietta Leavitt's work on a strange kind of star called a cepheid variable. A variable is a star that brightens and darkens, and, in the case of a cepheid, this happens because the star swells and shrinks. Some cepheids take a day or so to brighten and fade and brighten again (this the period of the cepheid), while others take months.

Leavitt studied thousands of them, and found that the brighter the cepheid, the longer its period. This was useful to Hubble because it meant he could measure distances to spiral nebulae.

Hubble found that the spiral nebulae are millions of light years away, far beyond the outer limits of our Milky Way Galaxy. In fact, he realized, they are galaxies themselves. Suddenly, the Universe had become a

much larger place.

Speak like a scientist

GALAXY

A group of thousands or millions of stars, held together by gravity. Our own galaxy is called the Milky Way Galaxy.

HEROES OF THE UNIVERSE

HENRIETTA LEAVITT

Found a way to measure distances across the Milky Way and beyond.

Hubble also recorded the spectra of these spiral nebulae, which he now knew were spiral galaxies, and found to his surprise that most of them are redshifted, due to the Doppler Effect (pages 29–30). This means they are moving away from our own galaxy at many hundreds of miles a second. With fellow astronomers Vesto Slipher and Milton Humason, Hubble found that the more distant a galaxy is, the larger its redshift. And it wasn't long before other astronomers realized what this meant:

the Universe is expanding!

HEROES OF THE UNIVERSE

EDWIN HUBBLE

Proved there are other galaxies, and helped discover that the Universe is expanding.

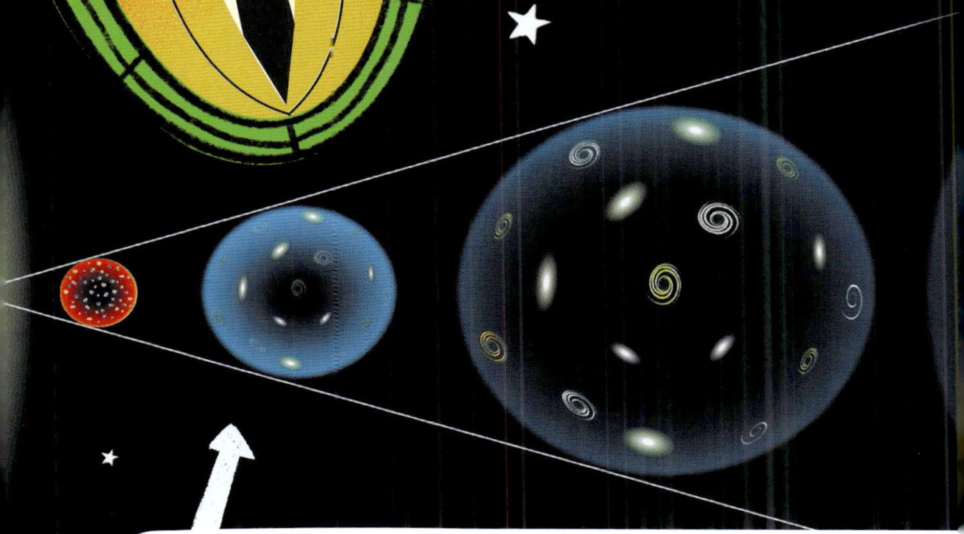

The circular shapes are groups of galaxies, moving apart as the Universe expands. Pick one and imagine you live there: If you measure the speeds at which other groups are moving away from you, you will find that nearby ones are retreating more slowly than distant ones. This is what Hubble measured.

The Cosmic Microwave Background

Saying that the Universe is expanding is the same as saying that groups of galaxies are moving away from one another, which means that long ago they must have been very close together. How long ago? Answering this question gives the age of the Universe, which is now estimated at about 13.8 billion years.

By the 1960s, most cosmologists agreed that the Universe began with the sudden appearance of a burst of energy and has been expanding ever since. This is known as the Big Bang theory. But how to prove it?

One way was through spectroscopy—showing not only which elements are present in stars, but how much of each. The mix of hydrogen, helium, and another very light **element** called lithium, revealed by spectra, fitted very nicely with the idea that they had formed in the Big Bang.

Secondly, if the Universe began as a sudden burst of energy billions of years ago, some of that energy should still exist today in the form of radiation. The very early Universe was so crushed and dense that radiation could not travel through it but, sometime around its 380,000th birthday, it had un-crushed itself so much (thanks to its ongoing expansion) that the radiation was able to escape.

Originally, this radiation was infrared but it has gradually changed over its billions of years of travel and is now in the form of microwaves. These microwaves fill the Universe and are known as the Cosmic Microwave Background (**CMB**).

Even though some scientists were looking for it, the CMB was found by accident in 1965 by Arno Penzias and Robert Wilson, who were experimenting with a giant radio receiver originally used for communication with satellites. Local pigeons used the radio receiver for a different purpose . . .

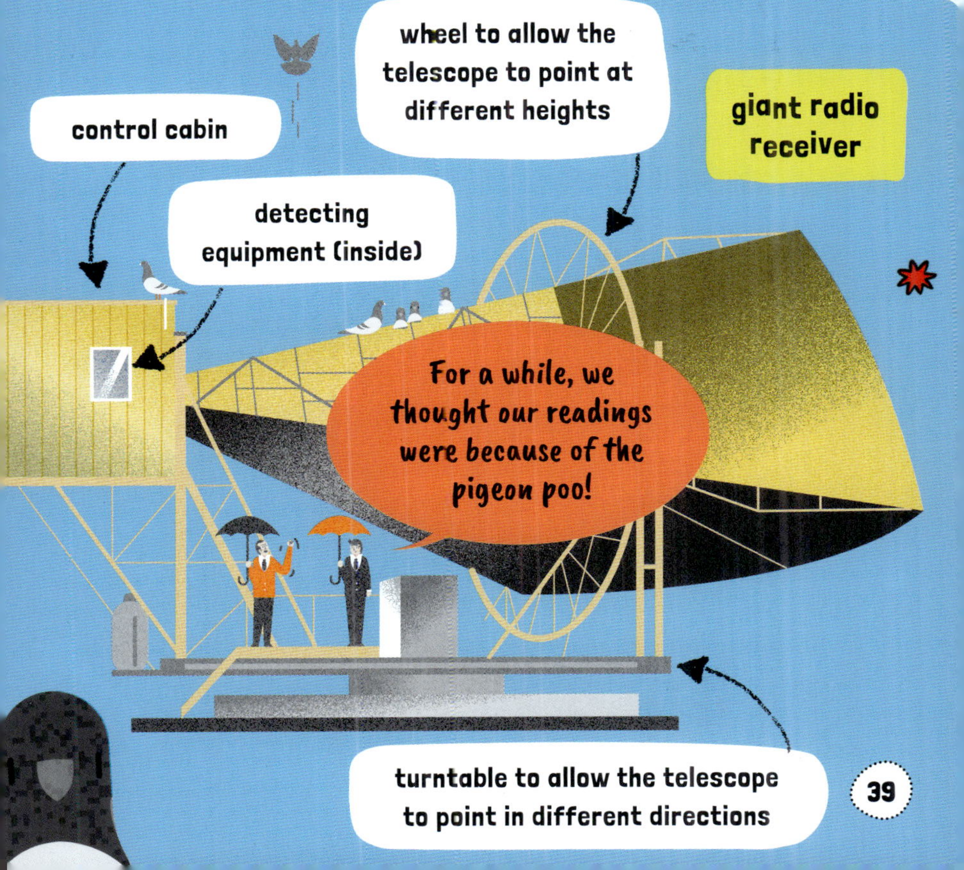

Mapping the early Universe

The burst of energy that began the Universe was not perfectly even. Some areas were a little hotter than the rest, with a bit more **matter** in them, and therefore more gravity. Over billions of years, the gravity of these hotter, denser areas attracted more matter toward them and slowly developed into galaxies, including our own. The traces of these hotspots are still there, in the CMB, which means that the long-gone early Universe has left us a map of itself. To read it, all we need are some (very accurate) microwave telescopes—in space. Three satellites have been built to map the CMB, each slightly better than the last, and the latest is called Planck.

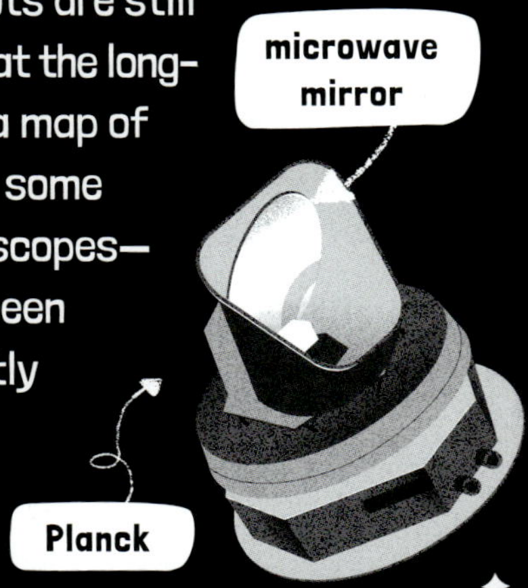

The maps the satellites made allowed astronomers to establish the age of the Universe as between 13.767 and 13.807 billion years. If the Universe was a ten-year-old child, that would be like estimating their age to within ten days just by looking at them.

13.8 billion years is unimaginably long. If time could be sped up into twelve months, the history of the Universe would look like this cosmic calender.

COSMIC CALENDAR

January BIG BANG	February	March Milky Way forms	April	May	June
July	**August**  Sun and planets form		**September** First life on Earth	**October**	**November** First complex cell life appears

DECEMBER

1	2	3	4	5	6	7
8	9	10	11	12	13	14 First animals
15	16	17 First fish	18	19	20 Land plants	21 Insects
22 Amphibians	23 Reptiles	24	25 Dinosaurs	26 Mammals	27 First birds	28 Flowers
29	30  Dinosaur extinction		31 First humans appear at eight minutes to midnight.			

The super-powerful telescopes that cosmologists use to study the Universe reveal a huge number of galaxies, each made up of a huge number of stars. The next chapter is all about them.

Chapter 5

The Lives of the Stars

If you use a bicycle pump, it warms up. This is because you are increasing the pressure of the air in it, and whenever pressure increases, heat is the result.

Stars are the same, except that their high gravity does the pushing rather than muscle power. This gravity means the pressure in the core (middle) of the star is very high, generating great heat.

When a gas gets hot, the tiny particles it is made of move faster. In the core of a star like the Sun, the particles are the **nuclei** (centers) of hydrogen atoms (nuclei is the plural of nucleus). At a temperature of several million degrees, some particles crash together so hard that they stick. This process, which is called **nuclear fusion**, forms helium nuclei and releases energy, including **lots of heat and radiation**, which we see as sunlight and starlight.

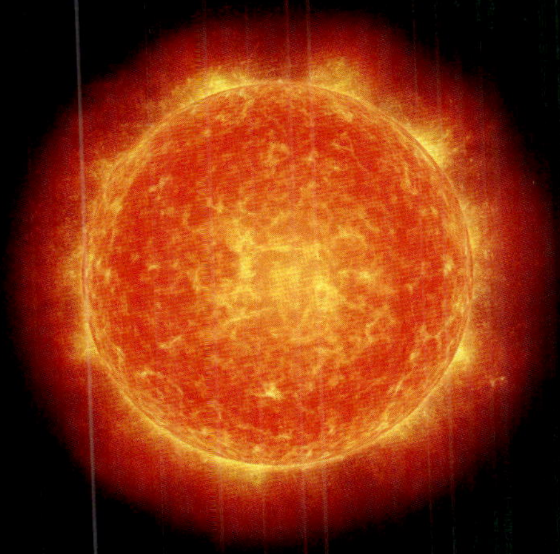

The flood of outrushing light and other radiation pushes outward on the star's outer layers. But these layers can't move far because the strong pull of the star's gravity holds them back. So, stars are the result of a balancing act between the inward pull of gravity and the outward push of pressure. This is similar to a balloon: The stretchy rubber is like the effect of gravity, trying to squeeze it smaller, but the pressure of the air inside the balloon stops it from actually collapsing, like the radiation pressure from within a star.

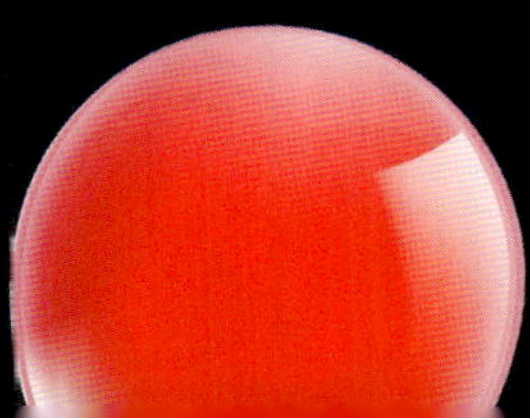

Speak like a scientist

ATOMS AND ELEMENTS

Every object in the Universe is made of atoms, which are tiny objects, far too small to see (there are more than a million trillion of them in a grain of sand). There are only about 100 different kinds of atom, and a substance made from just one kind of atom is called an element. Our bodies, for example, are mostly made of the elements carbon, hydrogen, and oxygen.

Part of a nebula where stars are forming, called **The Pillars of Creation**

Starbirth

The stars we can see today, and those being born now, form in the hearts of clouds of dust and gas. These clouds can exist for many millions of years without changing, until the gravity of a nearby star, either passing by or exploding, disturbs them. Gas and dust begin to swirl and become thicker in some places.

Each of the thick, swirling areas collapses under the pull of its own gravity, forming a huge, round clump called a protostar. The protostar keeps increasing in mass as new matter falls on to it, and this increases the pressure and temperature at its core. Eventually, the temperature is high enough for nuclear fusion to begin, and the star begins to shine brightly. In many cases, cloud material near the star forms into planets and smaller objects.

Life histories

All stars begin as protostars and all change as they age, but there are several different star life stories. The story of any star depends only on its mass.

The lives of stars

birth

old age

Turn the page to find out more . . .

1 In stars much more massive than the Sun, once all the hydrogen in the core has been used up, core temperatures can rise high enough for new kinds of fusion: Some helium nuclei fuse (join together) to become carbon nuclei, some of which then fuse to become oxygen nuclei and so on, until there are many different elements deep inside the star. When no more fusion is possible, the star stops producing radiation. As there is nothing to hold up the star's outer layers any more, they crash down and then explode. This is called a supernova and it can be brighter than an entire galaxy. The elements are scattered through space as cosmic dust and gases, and eventually become part of other stars, planets, and everything else, including you. Supernovae leave behind tiny shrunken cores with very strong gravity. These are either neutron stars or, if the original star was very high in mass, black holes. In a black hole, gravity is so strong that nothing can escape it—not even light.

2 The Sun, and other stars of similar mass, will one day become red giants. When their cores run out of hydrogen, hydrogen farther out begins to fuse and the star glows brighter, turns redder, and grows larger, swelling to engulf any inner planets (in our Solar System, this will happen in around five billion years). The outer layers go on spreading until the red giant has become a bubble of expanding gas called a planetary nebula, with a shrunken white dwarf star at its core. The white dwarf cools and fades to a black dwarf, but this is such a slow process that the Universe is still too young for any black dwarfs to have formed.

3 Lower-mass protostars become red dwarfs, which live a very long time until they run out of fuel and become white dwarfs.

4 The least massive protostars become brown dwarfs, objects partway between planets and stars and too small for fusion (when atomic nuclei are fused together to make new and different atoms) to take place.

The stars you can see on a clear night are scattered through space with no particular pattern. But if you flew a spacecraft for a few million years, you would see that in fact they are gathered together into the spiral pattern of the Milky Way Galaxy. If you kept going for a few more million years, what patterns and groupings would you see?

To find out, read on . . .

Chapter 6

Our Place in the Universe

On some dark and moonless nights, a long smear of faint light can be seen rising high up into the sky.

This is called the **Milky Way** and it is the closest part of our **Milky Way Galaxy**, a system of about 100 to 400 billion stars, of that the Sun is one. The part of the Milky Way that is visible from the Southern Hemisphere is brightest, because that is the direction of the center of the galaxy.

Even though light is fast, it takes nearly 200,000 years to cross the galaxy (though astronomers are unsure of the Milky Way's Galaxy exact size).

Photo of the Milky Way in the night sky taken with a special camera

Other galaxies

The observable Universe contains about two trillion (two million million) galaxies. The smallest galaxies contain less than a million stars, the largest more than a trillion. All of them are held together by gravity, and almost all have enormously massive black holes at their hearts: Our galaxy's central black hole is about four million times as massive as the Sun and is called Sagittarius A* (pronounced "A-star").

There are six types of galaxy:

1 SPIRAL

2 BARRED SPIRAL

3 LENTICULAR

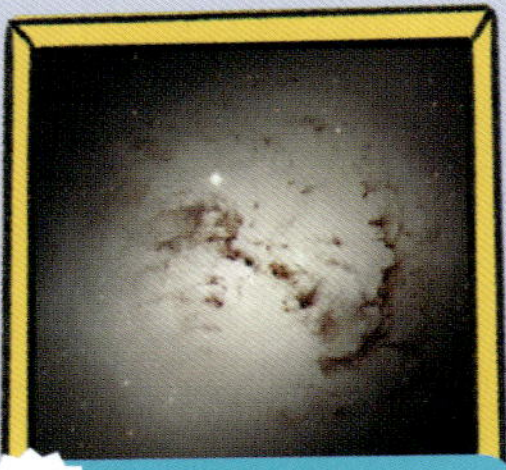

4 ELLIPTICAL

5 IRREGULAR

6 INTERACTING

1 About two-thirds of the galaxies we can see are spirals, which are disk-shaped, with a central bulge and spiral arms.

2 Many spirals, including the Milky Way Galaxy, have long bars of stars at the center and are called "barred spirals."

3 Lenticular galaxies are lens-shaped (or lentil-shaped, which is what "lenticular" means) with central bulges but no spiral arms.

4 Elliptical galaxies have no arms, and range in shape from globe-shaped to baguette-shaped. Giant elliptical galaxies may contain more than a trillion stars and be two million light years across.

5 Irregular galaxies have no particular shape, often because they have been pushed and pulled about by the gravities of other galaxies close by.

6 Interacting galaxies have complicated shapes and are the result of galaxies merging.

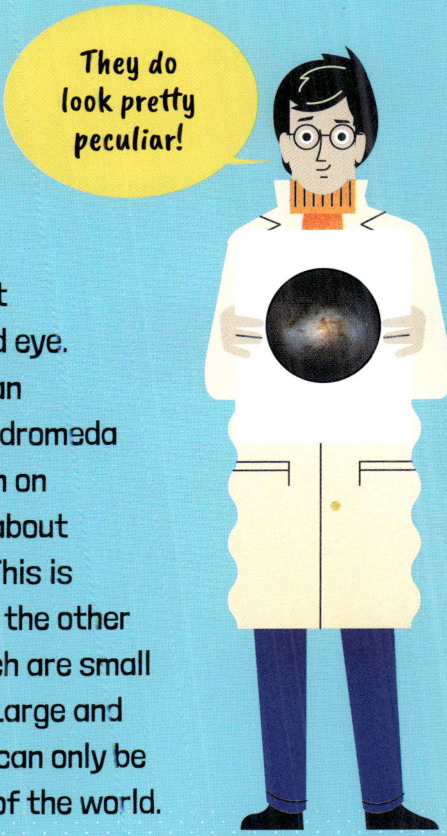

Galaxies are the most distant objects visible with the naked eye. In the Northern Hemisphere, an enormous spiral called the Andromeda Galaxy can just about be seen on the blackest of nights—it is about 2.5 million light years away. This is about ten times farther than the other two naked-eye galaxies, which are small irregular galaxies called the Large and Small Magellanic Clouds that can only be seen from the southern half of the world.

The Sun, and all the individual stars we can see using only our eyes, lie within a tiny region of the Orion spiral arm of the Milky Way Galaxy. Our galaxy probably has three other spiral arms, but this is uncertain because we cannot properly see much of it, partly because there are many dark nebulae that interrupt our view.

Galaxies in groups

Some galaxies drift through space alone, but most are members of groups; a group with more than about fifty large galaxies is called a cluster.

The Milky Way Galaxy, together with the three galaxies we can see using our eyes, and about fifty more, form the not-very-excitingly-named Local Group.

Gravity links all the galaxies in a group, just as it links the Sun and planets to make the Solar System. But while the planets settled into their orbits around the Sun billions of years ago, many galaxies in groups are still shifting their arrangements, even though they have been on the move almost since the Universe began. For instance, in the Local Group, the Andromeda Galaxy is approaching our own and will merge with it in about 4.5 billion years, forming a giant new galaxy.

In the largest clusters, billions of years of galactic mergers have led to the formation of huge elliptical galaxies. The Coma Cluster, for example, includes NGC 4874, a galaxy more than ten times the size of the Milky Way Galaxy. (Despite its mammoth size and interestingness, no one has got around to naming it properly: NGC just stands for "New General Catalogue.")

Superclusters and beyond

The Local Group together with about a hundred other groups and clusters of galaxies form a structure called a supercluster. It is called the Virgo Supercluster because it has a large central cluster (also called Virgo, confusingly) that is in the same direction as the constellation of Virgo. However, this cluster is millions of times farther from us than the stars in that constellation.

The gravitational pull between different clusters is very feeble, not enough to pull superclusters into any particular shapes—and, elsewhere in the Universe, clusters are arranged in many other ways, including fairly flat sheets and long thin strands called filaments. All these shapes have sizes so vast they are measured in

hundreds of millions of light years.

About 100 superclusters and other large structures have so far been identified, and there are thought to be about ten million in the observable Universe. Between them are **huge gulfs** of space called voids, which, apart from a very few lost and lonely galaxies, are almost completely empty. This random jumble is called the **Cosmic Web.**

Superclusters and the like are the biggest things in the Universe. They are too dim to see with the naked eye, but if you could see all the hundred or so we know of, and then zoomed out, you would simply see more and more of them, until each was too tiny to see. The Universe at this scale would look like a very dimly glowing fog, with no patterns or structures at all. Zooming out even farther would not change this view.

Einstein's Universe

If you could explore the entire Universe in a spacecraft, you would never reach an end, or an edge or boundary of any kind. In a way, this is like exploring Earth.

No matter how far you go, you will never reach an end.

No existing spacecraft could explore in this way though, so it's good that Albert Einstein found a way to explore the Universe mathematically instead.

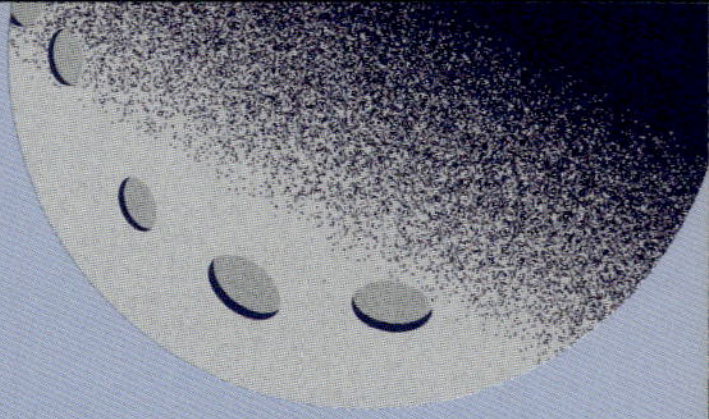

Einstein found that time is slowed by gravity. If you lived on the Moon, where gravity is lower than on Earth, your watch would go a little faster than on Earth and you would age just a little faster than a twin you left at home. On the other hand, if you lived near a black hole, you would hardly age at all.

Gravity changes space, as well as time. Some of the most distant things we can see are intensely bright objects called **quasars**. A quasar is an extremely **massive** black hole onto which an enormous amount of matter is constantly falling. The light comes from the matter as it reaches very high temperatures just before disappearing into the black hole.

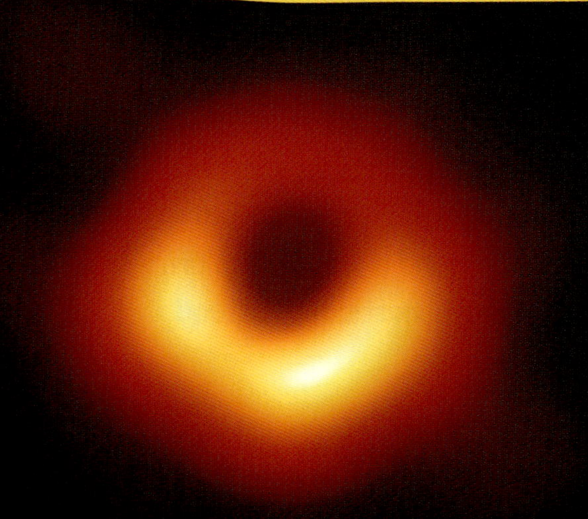

Black hole with a ring of very hot, glowing matter around it.

One quasar happens to lie behind a galaxy—but we can still see it because the gravity of the galaxy makes the light curve around itself. Actually, we can see four images of the quasar because of the complicated way the light curves. The galaxy acts as a lens—this is called gravitational lensing.

This quadruple quasar is called Einstein's Cross, because Einstein showed that the simplest way to think of gravity is as a curve in space caused by the presence of mass. There are other crosses like this in the Universe, and other, milder, forms of gravitational lensing too.

The idea that the space we live in could be curved gets easier if we try to think of the Universe as if it has no height. Then, the curves made by massive objects like stars would be deep depressions (called gravity wells).

This gives us a new way of thinking about gravity and its effects: Instead of saying that a star's gravity pulls a spacecraft passing by, now we can see that the spacecraft will tend to slide down the curved sides of the well and would need to power up its engine to escape.

How gravity works

(NOT to scale)

We're going down a gravity well!
I don't think you appreciate the gravity of the situation!

Since mass curves space, and since the Universe is very massive, the space it occupies might be very curved. Could there be enough mass to curve space so much that the Universe is a bit like the inside surface of a ball? In other words, do we live in a closed Universe? This is hard to imagine, and even harder to answer—at the moment, we just don't know.

Now you know everything (well, almost) about the **fantastically, startlingly enormous** Universe. But it hasn't always been this big—in fact it hasn't always been here.

So, disembark from your imaginary superfast spacecraft, fire up your imaginary time machine, and take a trip back through **several billion years of time.**
Or alternatively, just read the next chapter.

Chapter 7

Since the Beginning

Thanks to observations of distant galaxies and the Cosmic Microwave Background, and the work of Einstein and others, the story of our Universe could at last be told. So, 13.8 billion years ago . . .

The Big Bang and after

The Universe began with the sudden appearance and instant expansion of a vast amount of energy at an extremely high temperature. But this was not an explosion: An explosion happens when the parts of an object are violently flung out into the surrounding space, but when the Universe began there was no space to explode into.

Speak like a scientist

ENERGY AND MATTER

Energy includes heat, light, sound, electricity, motion, mass, and many other similar things.

Continued . . .

ENERGY AND MATTER

(continued)

Matter is anything that takes up space and has mass (which is closely related to weight). The solids, liquids, and gases we see around us are all different kinds of matter.

Solid things like ice cubes melt into liquid and boil into gas when they are heated (heating is one way of adding energy to matter). Given a high enough temperature, all solid things would become gases. At even higher temperatures a gas changes again, as its atoms break apart (this is a fourth state of matter called a plasma). Even these pieces of atoms cannot survive if the temperature is high enough and they are destroyed, too.

At the temperature of the Big Bang, it was too hot for any of the particles we know today to exist. The super-energetic particles that existed then were unimaginably strange.

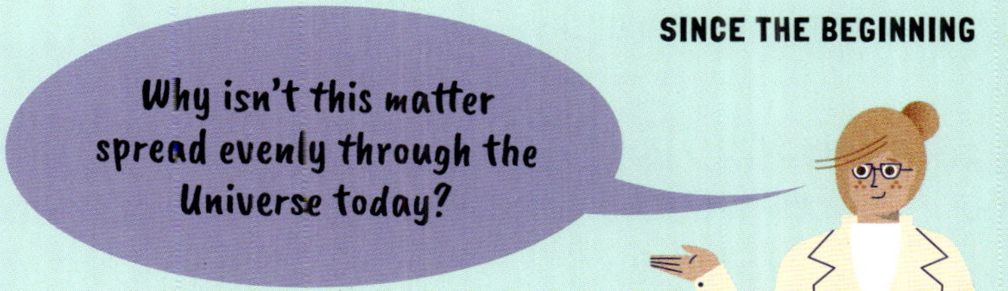

Mysteries from the beginning of time

One of the strangest things about our strange Universe is that it contains stars. Since everything began as a sudden burst of energy, a little of which turned into matter, it raises some tricky questions for cosmologists.

Trying to solve this and other mysteries has led most cosmologists to accept that something called inflation happened in the very early Universe, before matter began to form. Inflation was a sudden enormous increase in how fast the Universe was expanding, which slowed down again almost as soon as it had begun.

This would have allowed tiny random hot and cold spots in the pattern of energy, which would otherwise have faded away immediately, to survive (we met them on page 40). These areas would eventually become galaxies.

Speak like a scientist

PARTICLES

Inside every atom are a number of smaller particles, and there are three main kinds: heavy particles called **neutrons** and **protons**, which are locked tightly together in the atom's nucleus, and lighter particles called **electrons**, which move around the nucleus.

Electrons each carry a tiny electric charge, and it is the electrons flowing along a wire that we call electric current, used to make light bulbs, phones, and most other machines work.

Electrons can easily be stripped from atoms (it happens when you take off your jumper and it crackles with static, and when you switch on a light, sending electrons moving down the wires).

Atomic nuclei can be pulled apart too, although this is much more difficult (that happens in the nuclear reactions that go on inside stars and in nuclear power stations on Earth).

As far as we know, it is impossible to pull apart an electron. We can't pull apart neutrons or protons either, but at the incredible temperatures very soon after the Big Bang, this could be done: The particles that neutrons and protons are made of are called quarks (three quarks are needed to make one neutron or proton).

Like electrons, quarks can't (as far as we know) be broken down into smaller particles. If electrons or quarks are destroyed, they just turn into energy. Some scientists think that this energy behaves like tiny patterns of vibration, called strings.

Within a **millionth of a second** of the beginning of the Universe, temperatures had fallen enough that some of the energy of the Big Bang could turn into particles of matter, including electrons and quarks.

Positrons and anti-quarks appeared, too. These are types of **antimatter**. Antimatter has some properties that are the opposite of ordinary matter.

For instance, electrons are negatively charged but positrons are positive. Negative and positive electric charges are sort of like the north and south poles of a magnet. Just like the south pole of a magnet will attract (pull) the north pole of another magnet, an electron will attract a positron. And, just like one north pole will repel (push away) another north pole, electrons push each other away.

If the north pole of a magnet is allowed to touch the south pole of another, nothing very exciting happens—the magnets just stick together. But when a positron meets an electron, both **vanish in a flash** of radiation (this is called **annihilation**, which is from a Greek phrase meaning "to become nothing"). The reverse happens too: In laboratories, when atoms are smashed together at enormous speeds they release a great deal of radiation, and from this radiation, pairs of electrons and positrons can appear.

This appearance of particles from high-energy radiation is exactly what happened just after the

BIG BANG.

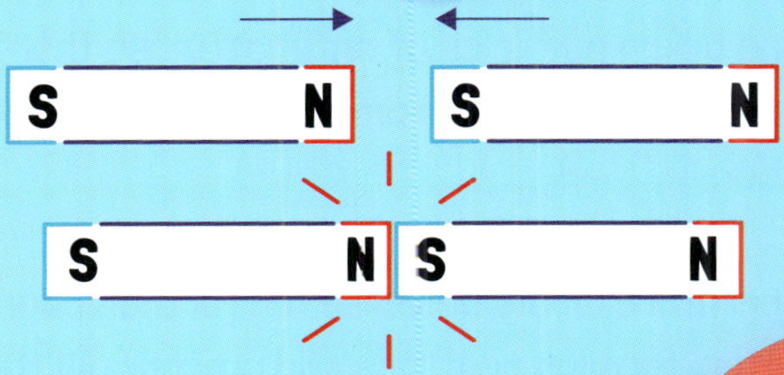

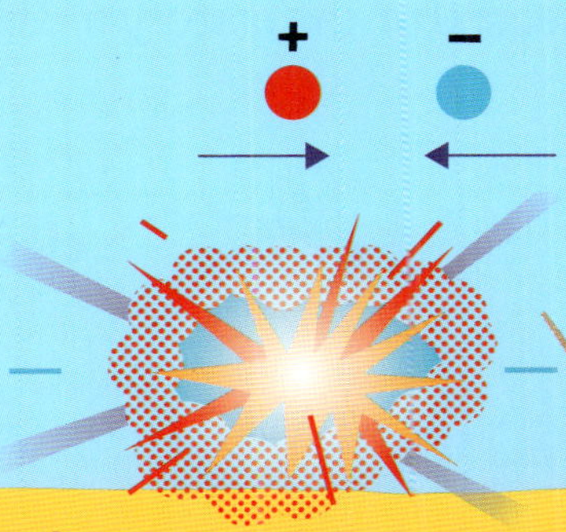

Opposite magnetic poles attract and snap together. **Electrons** and **positrons** (anti-electrons) attract and go **BANG!!!**

Less than a second after all these particles and antiparticles had appeared, almost every one of the new particles of matter had encountered an antimatter particle, and they had destroyed each other.

Mysteriously, but very luckily for us, the Universe originally had about one billion and one matter particles for every one billion particles of antimatter, so there was a little matter left over from this enormous storm of destruction.

As the temperature of the Universe fell further, quarks joined together, forming neutrons and protons. All this happened in the first second of the history of the Universe.

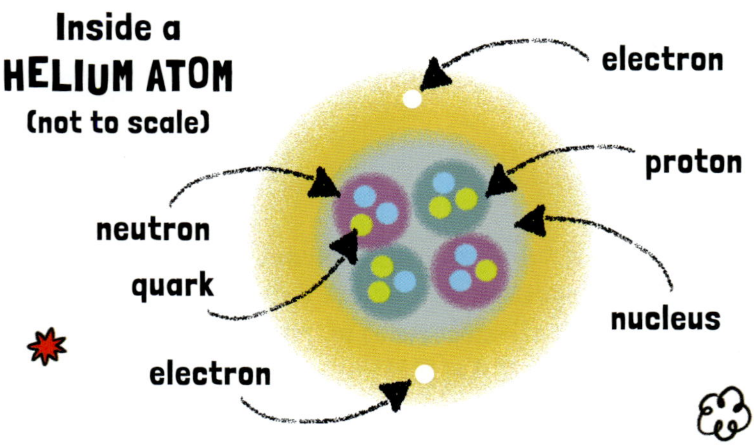

Three minutes later, some of the neutrons and protons had joined to form helium nuclei (which are made up of two protons and two neutrons). Other protons remained separate, as did all the electrons.

For 380,000 years, the Universe was too hot for these particles to develop any further, but it was cooling all the time. Finally, when the Universe had cooled to about 3,000 K, electrons could stick to the helium nuclei to form helium atoms and to the protons to form hydrogen atoms (a hydrogen atom's nucleus is just a proton).

Until now, although the Universe had been packed with high-energy radiation, it was also stuffed full of so many particles that this radiation was trapped. But, as the electrons became parts of atoms, this radiation was set free.

This radiation was infrared at the time, but it has long since turned into microwaves: the CMB we met on pages 38–39.

So, the oldest radiation that we can possibly detect comes from about 380,000 years **after the Big Bang**. Can we ever look back to an earlier time than this? Thanks to gravitational waves (see page 26), perhaps we can. They could travel through the earliest moments, so that one day, when we build good enough detectors, we may be able to peer back almost to the Big Bang.

Dark matter in a dark Universe

After about a few hundred thousand years, the Universe had cooled so much that all the light had changed to infrared.

For at least 150 million years after that, the Universe was absolutely dark. But where the inflationary period had left hotspots, a little extra matter had gathered. We don't know what kind of matter this was, but we do know that it neither shines, nor reflects light, so it is called dark matter. It forms most of the matter in every galaxy today.

In fact, most of the matter in the Universe is of this strange type. Like all matter, it attracts other matter with the force of gravity. So, the places where dark matter was thickest pulled gently on the atoms that floated around them, drawing them in.

This process sped up as those atoms that drifted into these denser areas added their own tiny gravity pulls, which attracted even more atoms, increasing gravity further, and so on.

Eventually these areas were packed with moving atoms. As they jostled and banged into each other, the temperature rose (that's what heat is: the rushing about of particles). It would never again reach the levels of the Big Bang, but eventually it became hot enough for the gas to start glowing a dim deep red.

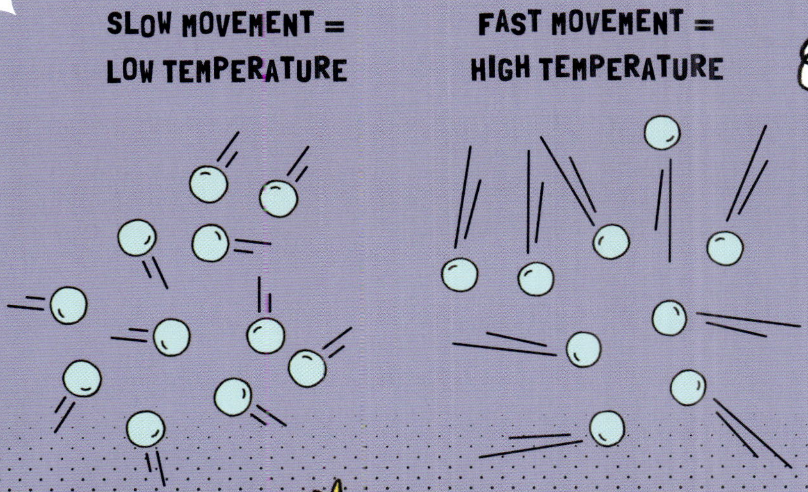

The lost stars

The hydrogen inside us was made in the Big Bang, but the carbon, oxygen, and other elements were made inside massive stars, which then spread out into space as the stars exploded as supernovae.

A star spends most of its life fusing hydrogen to helium. Only toward the end of a massive star's life, when the hydrogen begins to run out, do other elements start to form.

Yet the Sun's spectral lines show that it contains small amounts of these other elements too. In fact, every single star we can study contains them. But the Sun, and most other stars, are too young and low in mass to have made them.

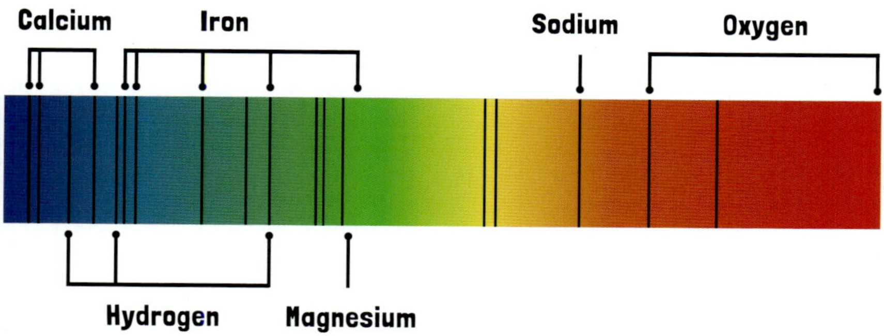

The only explanation seems to be that all stars formed from material that already contained these elements.

So where did these elements come from to begin with? Cosmologists think there must once have been stars that were made only of hydrogen and helium, with no other elements at all. It must have been the most massive of these stars that, toward the ends of their lives, made the other elements and then spread them out through space when they exploded as supernovae.

This nebula is the leftovers of a supernova (with added color).

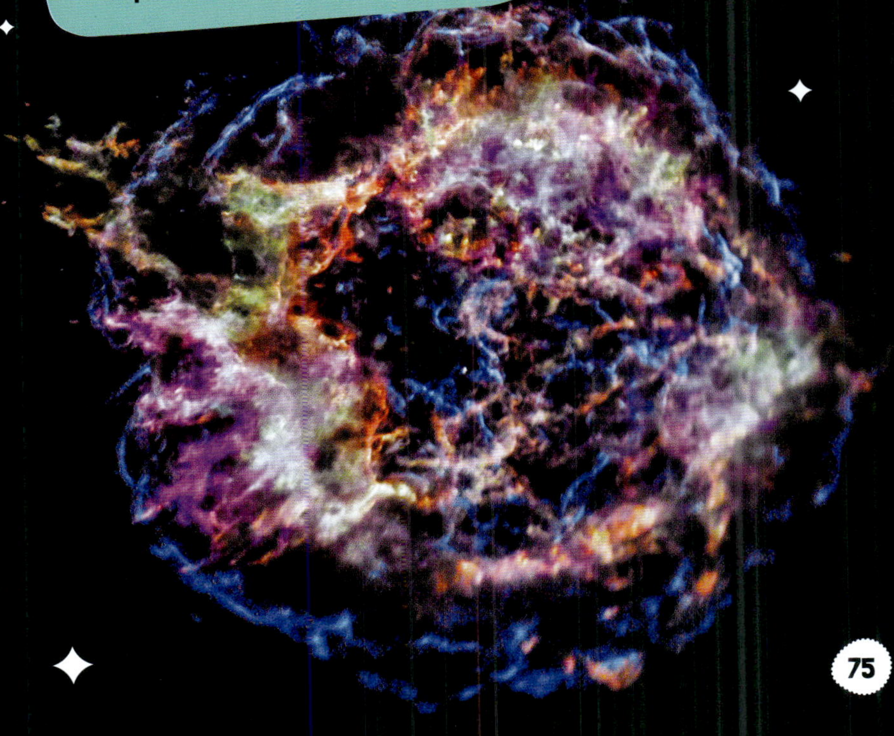

These hydrogen-and-helium-only stars are called Population III (pronounced "three") stars. The strange thing is, despite many searches over many years, not a single Population III star has ever been found. This is odd because stars live a long time: Most stars have lower masses than the Sun, and these low-mass stars live longest. A star of half the mass of the Sun will live for over 50 billion years, for instance, while the Universe is only 13.8 billion years old. It may be that all Population III stars had high masses and therefore short lives, but it's hard to see why this should be.

For the moment, it's one of the Universe's many mysteries.

The birth of worlds

As this first generation of stars in the Universe died, they spread the new elements they had made throughout their home galaxies in the form of cosmic dust and gas. Gradually, vast dark clouds grew and thickened. Many would become the birthplaces of a new generation of stars.

Dust and gas clouds in a **nebula**, where stars are born

PROTOSTAR

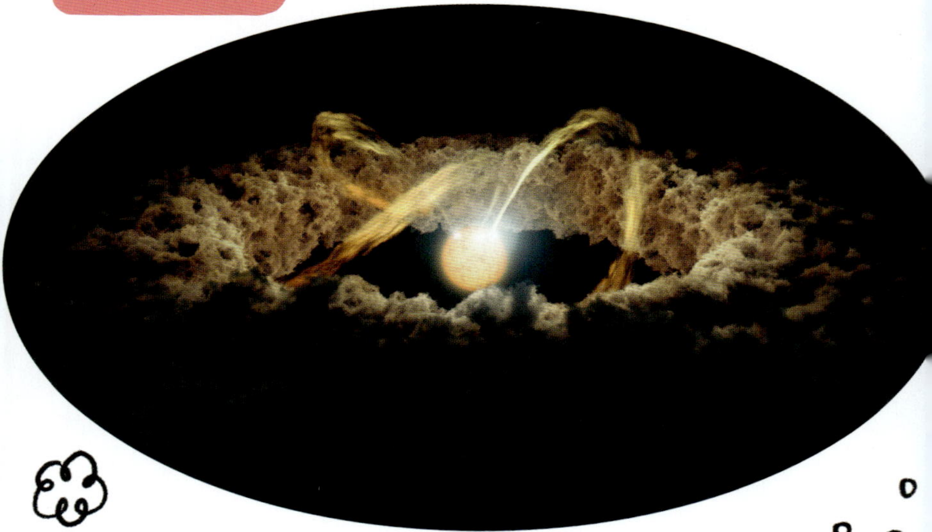

Many, perhaps most, of this new generation of stars had planets, which formed from billions of orbiting dust particles that surrounded the stars, making disks.

Why did these disks form? The stirring of the cloud that started the clumping process meant that there were trillions of dust grains rushing around at high speeds.

Imagine one of these dust grains speeding past a protostar.

The protostar's gravity will pull on the grain which will then move toward the protostar . . .

. . . but its speed means it will start to orbit the protostar instead of crashing into it. This is exactly how spacecraft are sent into orbit around other planets.

Our own Solar System formed about 4.6 billion years ago, which is about 9.2 billion years after the Big Bang, but the first planetary systems formed billions of years earlier—possibly just a few hundred million years after the Big Bang.

THE HISTORY OF THE UNIVERSE

TIME SINCE BIG BANG (APPROXIMATELY)	WHAT HAPPENED?
0	The Big Bang: Time, space, and energy appeared.
1 trillionth of a yoctosecond (a yoctosecond is a trillionth of a trillionth of a second)	Sudden short rapid expansion (inflation)
1 trillionth of a second	Particles of matter and antimatter formed; most destroyed each other.
1 millionth of a second	Neutrons, protons, and other particles formed from the remaining matter.
380,000 years	Atoms formed and infrared appeared (it has become the CMB).
200 million years	First stars formed.
9.3 billion years	Solar System formed.

So, now you know what's been happening everywhere for the last few billion years.

What will the next **trillion trillion trillion** years be like? We don't really know, but the next chapter has some ideas.

Chapter 8

The End of the Universe

At the moment, the Universe is expanding: The clusters of galaxies are all rushing away from one another. However, the clusters are also pulled toward each other with the force of their gravity, so this must be slowing them down. It may be that this gravity will eventually make them stop, and then pull them all back together again. This would mean the Universe stops expanding and starts to contract.

On the other hand, if they are going fast enough, the clusters may keep going forever, always slowing down, but never actually stopping. This would mean the expansion of the Universe continues.

By the 1990s, cosmologists knew how fast the Universe was expanding, but not its rate of slowdown. If they could measure how fast the Universe was expanding billions of years ago, they could compare that with today's slowed-down-by-gravity expansion rate.

To find out, a group of fifty-six cosmologists teamed up to observe some very distant supernovae.

But the results were incredible: Ancient supernovae are (or were) moving ***slower*** than recent ones.

Which means the expansion of the Universe is speeding up!

This is still a major mystery, but it seems that most of the energy in our Universe works a bit like gravity in reverse, pushing instead of pulling. It is called dark energy. Within the Solar System, the push of dark energy can't be detected and gravity is the force that matters, but over the enormous distances between clusters of galaxies, it seems that dark energy can overcome the pull of gravity.

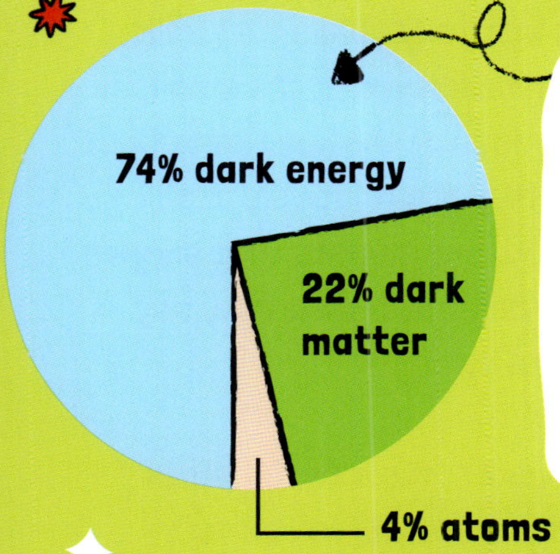

Most of the Universe is composed of things we know little about: dark matter and dark energy. Only 4% of it is the stuff that's made from atoms, stars, planets, dust, and all of us.

A hundred trillion years

The Universe is still very young (if it was a person it would be a newborn baby, less than a day old), and will remain more or less the same as it is today for many trillions of years. Over this immense and unimaginably long period, it will continue to expand, so each cluster of galaxies will move farther away from its neighbors, speeding up as it goes, until each cluster is alone in space. Within clusters, many galaxies will merge. And within the galaxies, stars will continue forming, growing old, and dying, and new stars and planets will be born from their remains. But eventually there will be no material left to form new stars. Dead stars will not be replaced and the Universe will grow darker.

The smallest stars will be last to go: While a star like the Sun lives for around ten billion years, the smallest kind (about one-tenth the mass of the Sun) last about 100 times longer. Because they are relatively cool, these small stars are red. So, any planets that survive into the distant future will be lit by red suns by day and red moons and red stars by night.

In about a hundred trillion years, the last red stars will have burned out and darkness will fall all over the Universe.

Three far futures

The future of our Universe after the death of the last stars is very uncertain and we need even more accurate measurements to make good predictions. But most cosmologists think there are three ways the Universe might end **(long, long after the time of *even* our grandchildren's grandchildren's grandchildren).**

1 Heat death (or "big chill")

The Universe will continue to expand forever, and all its dead stars will be swallowed up by black holes. For a long time, it was believed that black holes last forever, but Stephen Hawking proved that they will eventually all destroy themselves, losing mass in the form of "Hawking radiation," and finally exploding. After the black holes are all gone, there will just be a very thin sprinkling of particles and photons left in the Universe.

HEROES OF THE UNIVERSE

STEPHEN HAWKING

Discovered how black holes die.

2 Big Rip

There are several theories about how dark energy works. One predicts that the expansion of the Universe will start to affect smaller and smaller objects. As a result, the galaxies in clusters will move away from each other and then fall apart, turning into spreading clouds of stars. Then, those stars will lose their planets as the expansion of space continues to affect ever-smaller distances. Eventually, every star and then every world and, in the very distant future, every atom will be ripped to shreds. Even space and time will shatter one day—and that day will be the last of all.

3 Big Crunch

The expansion of the Universe will slow down, stop, and then collapse in on itself until it's very dense, very hot, and very small—as it was when it began. This might be followed by a "Big Bounce"—a new Big Bang and a new Universe. If this is possible, then perhaps our own Universe is just the most recent in a whole series of Universes, looping through an everlasting cycle of Big Bang, Big Crunch, and Big Bang again. However, the constant outward push of dark energy means the Big Crunch is the least likely end of the Universe.

Cosmologists have done an amazing job in working out so much about the Universe, its past and its future. But, since the Universe is so big and weird, there are plenty of things they still don't know (which is what makes their job so much fun). Find out a few things that are left on their to-do lists in the final chapter.

Chapter 9

Cosmic Mysteries

The Universe is so vast and complex that it is amazing we have been able to find out so much about it. But many questions remain unanswered, including the secrets of dark matter and dark energy. "Why was there a Big Bang?" is probably the biggest question of all, but there seems no way to answer that at the moment. So, if you want to be a famous cosmologist, here are a couple of mysteries you might want to solve.

Is there life elsewhere?

It seems almost certain that life exists elsewhere in the Universe: Even in our own tiny Solar System there could be alien life, perhaps in underground oceans on the icy moons of Jupiter or under the dry riverbeds of Mars. And we know from Earth's history that living things are really just packages of complicated chemicals.

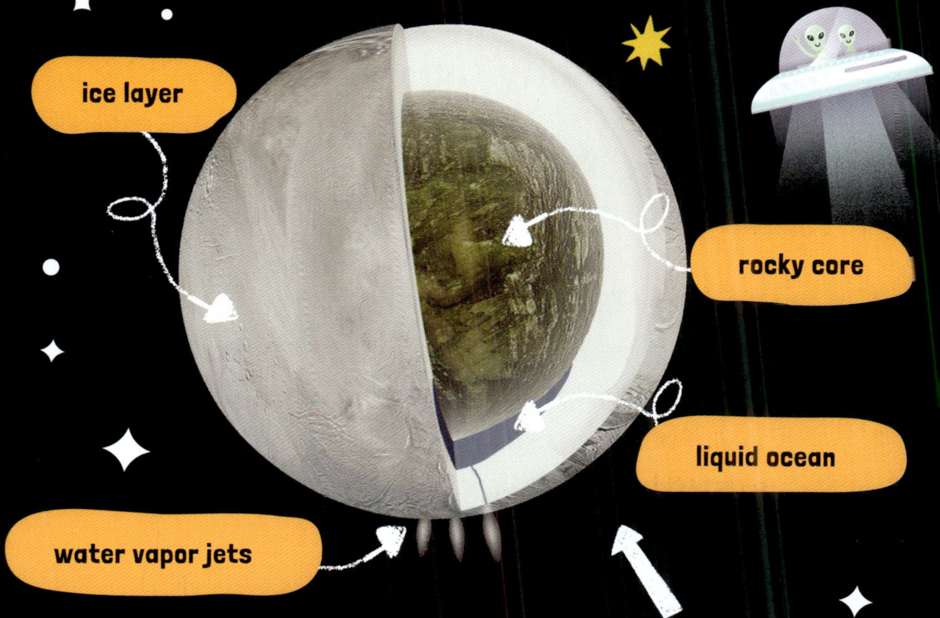

Water and other materials from Enceladus' hidden ocean burst out as jets of vapor from the surface, called plumes.

We can be fairly sure that civilizations like our own do not exist within many thousands of light years, or we would have detected their radio signals by now. On the other hand, the Universe is vast, so there are many places where intelligent creatures might be, in places too far for signals to reach. And the Universe is only a tiny part of the way through its history; there are many trillions of years left for intelligent life to evolve.

Is this the only Universe?

Could there by other Universes? That is, places we could never reach, no matter how far we traveled?

Whether other Universes exist depends partly on which of our theories about our own are correct. For instance, if the Big Bounce theory (page 86) is the true story of our Universe, then other Universes likely existed before ours was born and will exist after it has ended.

If our Universe has enough matter to be closed (page 62), then many other closed Universes might exist in the space outside it.

Or, other Universes might be hidden, if space has extra **dimensions**. A fourth dimension of space is hard to imagine, but picture yourself as one of the insects that lives on the surface of water, like a backswimmer. Your whole world is the flat (two dimensional) water surface. But really there is a **different and much bigger world below you,** which you cannot reach because you **cannot move downward.**

It *may* be that these mysteries will be solved in **your** lifetime. Perhaps **you** will help solve them yourself: There are many kinds of cosmologists, from satellite engineers to mathematicians, and from chemists to computer programmers. And nowadays, breakthroughs are made more often by teams of these experts than by individuals.

The Universe is an amazing and exciting place, full of mysteries and wonders:

But perhaps the most amazing and exciting thing about it is that

one day we *might* understand it ALL.

	DISTANCE FROM EARTH
Moon	1.3 light seconds
Sun	8.3 light minutes
Neptune (furthest planet in our Solar System)	4.0 light hours
Nearest star (Proxima Centauri)	4.2 light years
The center of our Milky Way Galaxy	2.6 thousand light years
Andromeda Galaxy (nearest large galaxy)	2.5 million light years
Virgo Supercluster (neighboring supercluster)	65.2 million light years
Hydra Supercluster (neighboring supercluster)	105 million light years

Glossary

antimatter a type of matter whose atoms have some opposite properties to ordinary matter. When matter and antimatter meet, huge amounts of energy are released

astronomer someone who studies the stars and other objects in space

atom a tiny object that makes up every kind of solid, liquid, and gas. It consists of a tiny, very dense nucleus surrounded by one or more electrons.

billion one thousand million (1,000,000,000)

black hole an object in which the density is so high that its gravity is too strong for anything, even light, to escape

CMB the Cosmic Microwave Background radiation, which fills the whole Universe

constellation an area of the sky containing a pattern of stars that is thought to resemble an animal, god, or other object. The sky is divided into 88 constellations

cosmology the study of the Universe

density a measure of how much mass there is in a particular space or object

dimension a direction, like up-and-down or left-and-right. Time is also a dimension

Doppler Effect the reddening of an object as it moves away, used to measure the object's speed (an approaching object becomes bluer)

electromagnetic spectrum radio waves, microwaves, infrared, light, ultraviolet, X-rays, and gamma rays

electron a particle that carries an electric charge. Atoms contain electrons, and moving electrons provide electricity

element a substance made of only one kind of atom. There are just over 100 elements, including hydrogen, gold, and iron

energy the power that makes things happen. Heat, light, sound, motion, electricity, magnetism, and mass are all kinds of energy

fusion (nuclear) the merging of the nuclei of atoms, to produce larger nuclei and energy. Nuclear fusion is the process that makes sunlight, starlight, and most elements

galaxy a group of thousands, millions, or billions of stars, held together by gravity

gravity (also called gravitation) the force (pull) with which every piece of matter in the Universe attracts every other piece

kelvin the Celsius (°C) and Fahrenheit (°F) scales we use today were invented before temperature was properly understood. The kelvin (K) scale is often used in cosmology, because it is related to energy. Something with no heat energy has a temperature of 0 on the kelvin scale. To convert from kelvins to °C, just subtract 273.5. To convert to °F, the formula is °F= (K – 273.15) x 9/5 + 32

light year the distance light travels in one year

mass the type of energy that, on Earth, we feel as weight

matter anything that takes up space and has mass—solids, liquids, and gases are all types of matter

nebula (plural nebulae) a cloud-like object in space

neutron one of the particles in the nucleus of an atom

neutron star a star with a tiny shrunken core, primarily made of neutrons, that forms after a supernova. It has very strong gravity

nuclear to do with the nuclei of atoms

nucleus (plural nuclei) the central part of an atom

observable Universe the part of the Universe that could be seen with the best possible telescopes

orbit the path of one object around another in space

particle a tiny fragment, too small to see. Atoms, electrons, quarks, and protons are all particles

photon a particle of electromagnetic radiation

planetary system a star and the planets and smaller objects that orbit it—the Solar System is one

proton one of the particles in the nucleus of an atom. It has an electric charge

quasar the intensely bright core of a particular kind of galaxy. Quasars are some of the brightest things in the Universe and telescopes can see them over billions of light years away

radiation (electromagnetic) a type of energy that shines from an object, including light, radio waves, microwaves, infrared, ultraviolet, X-rays, and gamma rays

solar to do with the Sun

Solar System the Sun and all the planets and other objects that orbit it

spectrum (plural spectra) a bar of colored light, like a rainbow, produced by a star or by heated material. Lines running across the bar are caused by particular substances in the star or material (there are other kinds of spectrum, but this is the type in this book)

supernova an explosion that destroys a massive star

trillion one million million (1,000,000,000,000)

Index

A

alien life 88, 89
Andromeda Galaxy 53, 55, 92
antimatter 68, 70, 80
Aristarchus 11–13
Aristotle 11, 13
atom 32, 42, 44, 49, 64, 66–68, 70, 71, 73, 80, 83, 86

B

Big Bang 38, 41, 63, 64, 67–69, 71–74, 80, 86, 88
Big Bounce 86, 90
Big Crunch 86
Big Rip 86
black hole 26, 47, 48, 51, 58, 59, 85
blueshift 30, 31

C

cepheid variable 33–35
clusters 54–56, 81, 83, 84, 86
constellation 10, 55
Copernicus, Nicolaus 12, 13
Cosmic Microwave Background (CMB) 38–40, 63, 71, 80
Cosmic Web 56

D

dark energy 83, 86, 88
dark matter 72, 73, 83, 88
Doppler, Christian 29
Doppler Effect 29, 30, 36
dwarf (star) 46, 47, 49

E

Earth 4, 7, 9–18, 25, 27, 35, 41, 57, 58, 67, 88
Einstein, Albert 20, 24, 57–59, 63
electromagnetic spectrum 18, 24, 26
electron 66–71
element 38, 44, 48, 74–76
energy 19, 20, 24, 32, 38, 40, 42, 63–69, 71, 80, 83

G

galaxy types 52–55
Galilei, Galileo 13, 21, 22
gamma ray 24
geocentric 13
gravitational lensing 58, 59
gravitational waves 26, 71
gravity 7, 17, 18, 20, 35, 40, 42, 43, 48, 45, 51, 55, 56, 58–61, 73, 79, 81, 83
gravity well 59, 61

H

Hawking, Stephen 85
heat death 85
helium 7, 38, 42, 48, 70, 71, 74–76
Herschel, William 14, 18
Hubble, Edwin 33–37
Hubble Space Telescope (HST) 25
hydrogen 7, 28, 38, 42, 44, 48, 71, 74–76

I

inflation 65, 72, 80
infrared 18, 23–25, 39, 71, 72, 80

J

Jupiter 13, 15, 88

K

kelvin (K) 32
Kepler, Johannes 16, 17

L

Leavitt, Henrietta 33, 34, 36
light minute 4

light second 4, 92
light waves 19, 29, 30
light year 4–6, 14, 25, 35, 53, 56, 82, 89, 92
Local Group 54, 55

M

Mars 10, 14, 88
mass 18, 20, 45, 48, 49, 59, 62–64, 72, 74, 76, 84, 85
matter 40, 45, 58, 59, 63–65, 68, 70, 72, 73, 80, 90
Mercury 14
microwaves 19, 24, 38–40, 63, 71
Milky Way Galaxy 35, 36, 49–52, 54
Moon 4, 9, 10, 27, 58, 92

N

nebula 33–36, 44, 47, 49, 54, 57, 77
Neptune 14, 15, 92
neutron 66, 67, 70, 71, 80
neutron star 47, 48
Newton, Isaac 17, 22
nuclear fusion 42, 45

O

observable Universe 6, 51, 56

P

particle 24, 42, 64, 66–71, 73, 78, 80, 85
photon 24, 25, 85
Pickering, Edward 31
planet 7–14, 16, 17, 27, 41, 45, 48, 49, 55, 78–80, 83, 84, 86, 92
planetary nebula 47, 49
planetary system 14, 80
Population III star 76
positron 68, 69
proton 66, 67, 70, 71, 80
protostar 45, 46, 49, 78, 79

Q

quark 67, 68, 70
quasar 58, 59

R

radiation 18, 19, 23–25, 38, 39, 42, 43, 48, 68, 69, 71, 85
radio waves 19, 23, 24
red giant (star) 47–49
redshift 30, 31, 36

S

Saturn 15
Solar System 7, 14, 17, 18, 27, 48, 55, 80, 83, 88, 92
spectral lines 28, 30–32, 74
spectroscopy 29, 38
spectrum / spectra 17, 18, 28, 30, 31, 36, 38
spiral galaxy 36, 52, 53
spiral nebula 33–36
Sun 4, 9–14, 16, 17, 21, 28, 41, 42, 46, 48, 50, 51, 54, 55, 74, 76, 84, 92
superclusters 55–57, 92
supernova 47, 48, 74, 75, 82

T

telescope 6, 13, 15, 21–23, 25, 26, 33, 39, 40, 41

U

ultraviolet 18, 23–25
Uranus 14, 15

V

Venus 14
Virgo Supercluster 55, 92

W

Wollaston, William Hyde 28

X

X-ray 24

Introducing the Universe experts:

AUTHOR

DR. MIKE GOLDSMITH

Dr. Mike Goldsmith is a doctor of astrophysics and is a member of the Royal Astronomical Society. He works as a scientist as well as writing science books for readers ranging in age from toddlers to adults. His books have been published in 25 countries, with two of them shortlisted for the *Royal Society Prize for Science Writing*.

CONSULTANT

SUNNY VAGNOZZI

Sunny Vagnozzi is a cosmologist at the University of Cambridge, UK. He is working to answer questions about the origin of the Universe, what it is made of, and what its final fate will be.

VERY SHORT INTRODUCTIONS • FOR CURIOUS YOUNG MINDS •

Answering BIG questions about BIG topics